Understanding

BREAST DISORDERS

Mr Michael J. Dixon and
Dr Robert C.F. Leonard

Published by Family Doctor Publications Limited
in association with the British Medical Association

IMPORTANT NOTICE

This book is not designed as a substitute for personal medical advice but as a supplement to that advice for the patient who wishes to understand more about his or her condition.

Before taking any form of treatment YOU SHOULD ALWAYS CONSULT YOUR MEDICAL PRACTITIONER.

In particular (without limit) you should note that advances in medical science occur rapidly and some of the information contained in this booklet about drugs and treatment may very soon be out of date.

Family Doctor Publications, PO Box 4664, Poole Dorset BH15 1NN

Medical Editor: Dr Tony Smith
Consultant Editors: Chris McLaughlin/Sue Davidson
Cover Artist: Dave Eastbury
Medical Artist: Philip Wilson
Design: MPG Design, Blandford Forum, Dorset
Printing: Reflex Litho, Thetford, Norfolk, using acid-free paper

ISBN: 1 898205 68 X

Contents

Know your breasts

DEVELOPING AND CHANGING

The breasts start to develop very soon after conception and, to begin with at least, do so in the same way whether the baby is a boy or a girl.

Five or six weeks after a baby starts to grow, and while it is still only inches long, a ridge of tissue can be seen running from what will subsequently be the armpit to the groin. This ridge of tissue is called the 'milk line'.

Later, at about six months into the pregnancy, special secretory cells grow inwards from the baby's nipples, and channels (or ducts) are formed. By the time the baby is born, the breast anatomy is in place in basic form. In fact, some newborn babies have swollen or even inflamed breasts as a result of hormones passed to them through the placenta from their mothers.

Most girls' breasts start to develop between the ages of nine and eleven, but the process can begin earlier or later. Even when fully grown, the breasts are not capable of producing milk at this stage. It's not unusual for boys to experience some breast development during puberty as well, but this is only temporary and usually disappears within a year or two.

During pregnancy, a woman's breasts will get much bigger and may double their weight as milk-producing cells multiply and the system of ducts expands. The nipples get darker in colour and blood vessels become more prominent. All these changes take place in response to various hormones a woman produces while she is pregnant and most are only temporary. However, once the nipples have become darker they will stay that way because they now contain more pigment than previously.

As we age, all our body tissues

begin to lose their elasticity, and the breasts are no exception. They start to sag and, after the menopause, the fall in levels of the female hormone oestrogen causes the glands inside the breasts to shrink so they tend to get smaller.

INSIDE YOUR BREASTS

The easiest way to understand how

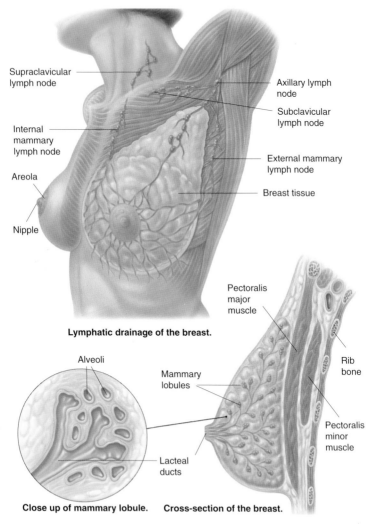

Supraclavicular lymph node

Axillary lymph node

Subclavicular lymph node

Internal mammary lymph node

External mammary lymph node

Areola

Breast tissue

Nipple

Lymphatic drainage of the breast.

Pectoralis major muscle

Alveoli

Mammary lobules

Rib bone

Lacteal ducts

Pectoralis minor muscle

Close up of mammary lobule. **Cross-section of the breast.**

Anatomy of the female breast.

the inside of the breast is formed is by comparing it to an upturned bush. Its 'leaves' are known as lobules. They produce milk which drains through the 'branches' along a network of small ducts. These in turn drain into 12 or 15 major or large ducts which then empty on to the surface of the nipple. The nipple is the equivalent of the bush's trunk. As with a bush, the breast's branching network of ducts is irregular and not arranged symmetrically like the segments of an orange.

The part of the breast most susceptible to disease is the lobules. There are not many conditions that affect the ducts, and the few that do involve the major ducts underneath the nipple.

The spaces you'd see in a bush between the leaves and the branches are filled inside the breast with connective tissue which plays a supporting role. Around all of this is a layer of fat between the milk-producing parts of the breast and the skin. The breasts are supported by the chest muscles beneath them, and toning up these muscles through the right kind of exercise is the only way to change your shape, apart from surgery. Exercise doesn't have any effect on the size or shape of the breast tissue itself.

BECOME 'BREAST AWARE'

Women used to be advised to examine their breasts carefully and regularly each month at the same point in their menstrual cycle. Not surprisingly, doing this made some women feel anxious and others felt guilty if they didn't do it and somehow responsible if they later developed a problem.

Today, most doctors agree that the really important thing is to know your own breasts so that you spot any unexpected change in them and can seek advice straightaway. This is called 'breast awareness'. What it means in practice is getting used to the appearance and texture of your breasts.

First, you should know what your breasts look like. It sounds obvious, but it's a good idea to get into the habit of looking at your breasts in the mirror from time to time after a shower/bath or when you're getting dressed. Notice how they move up as you raise your arms and so on – so that you know what's normal for you. What you are looking for is a change in the shape of the breast such as a pulling in of the skin, any visible swelling of the breast or a change in the nipple, such as a pulling in.

You also need to know how your breasts feel. No one could be expected to find a lump when feeling her breast for the first time. You need experience before you can judge what is normal for you. Most women's breasts are a bit lumpy,

CHECKING YOUR BREASTS

It is not recommended that you check your breasts regularly, but, if you wish to do so, a good time to do this is after a bath or shower when you're warm and relaxed. Start by using your right hand to feel your left breast, keeping your fingertips in line with your chest wall without digging them in. Remember to include the part of your breast that extends up into your armpit. Now do the same thing using your left hand on your right breast. What is more important than regular self-examination is to be aware of any change in the shape or feel of your breasts.

Look at your breasts for changes in appearance, size or the colour of the nipples

Raise your arms above your head. Turn to one side to see your breasts in profile; repeat your observations

Use your right hand to feel your left breast, keeping hand flat. Remember to include the armpit area

Now repeat the examination using your left hand to feel your right breast

especially during the few days before a period is due. After your period this lumpiness becomes less obvious or may well disappear altogether. Start by feeling your breasts every day for a few days until you're familiar with their texture and know how it changes through your menstrual cycle.

What if you find a problem?

You should see your doctor straightaway as soon as you notice any unusual change in your breasts – whether it's in the texture, the skin or the nipple. It's natural to feel anxious, but try to remember that roughly six out of seven breast lumps are NOT cancerous.

Even if you do turn out to have a serious problem, there is absolutely no doubt that early diagnosis and treatment greatly increases the chances that the cancer will be cured completely.

KEY POINTS

✓ Be aware of the shape and feel of your breasts

✓ Report any change in the shape of your breasts, or any lump that you feel, to your doctor

✓ Even if you find a lump, six of seven of these are not cancerous

Breast screening

Once a woman reaches the age of 50, she will be invited to take part in the National Breast Screening Programme. This means having a mammogram, a special kind of breast X-ray, once every three years. You will be invited until the age of 64, but screening will be extended to the age of 69 by 2003. If you want to continue to be screened every three years after the age of 70, you will need to make an appointment by phoning the screening unit or visiting the screening van when it is in your area. The aim of the programme is to pick up breast cancer while it is still small and before it has had a chance to spread.

There are various reasons why women are not normally screened before the age of 50:

- Breast cancer is less common in younger women.
- Mammography is less likely to detect abnormalities because young women's breast tissue is denser than that of older women.
- There is no evidence that screening women before they reach 50 is cost-effective.

However, younger women who are thought to be at particularly high risk of developing the condition for some reason (see pages 42–5) are often offered screening at an earlier stage in their lives. This is usually mammography performed more regularly than that in older women, although there is an ongoing study that is looking at whether a new type of scan (magnetic resonance imaging) is useful in screening young, high-risk women. In general, though, screening by regular mammograms is most effective in preventing death from breast cancer in women over the age of 50.

Women are currently screened every three years in the UK programme as this appears to be the 'best buy' from a cost-effectiveness point of view. However, some research suggests that doing it every two years would pick up more treatable cancers, so anyone who is offered more frequent mammograms, say at work, should accept.

WHAT HAPPENS WHEN YOU HAVE A MAMMOGRAM?

You will be asked to undress to the waist and stand in front of the X-ray machine. The radiographer will then position each breast in turn between two Perspex plates so that it is compressed and flattened. A brief pulse of X-rays is then used to take images of each breast – normally two per breast on the first visit and one or two on subsequent visits. Some women find the experience uncomfortable, and a few say that it is painful, but for the majority there's no more than minor discomfort. In any case, it's all over very quickly.

The X-ray film will then be examined and you will be told the results by your screening centre in around 10 days. A minority of women will be asked to return for a second mammogram, sometimes

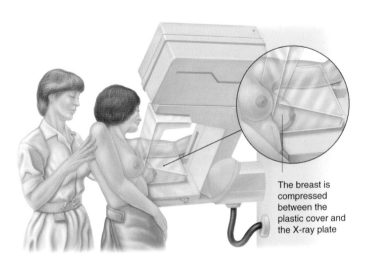

The breast is compressed between the plastic cover and the X-ray plate

A mammogram is a special kind of breast X-ray.

because something has shown up which needs further investigation or sometimes because of technical difficulties with the original X-ray. Remember that being recalled does not necessarily mean a diagnosis of cancer. Those who are recalled do see a doctor who will explain why the further check is needed.

What mammograms reveal

Although most women are reasonably happy to go for a routine mammogram, being asked to go back for a repeat test or further investigations is likely to make you anxious. This is natural enough, but it may help to keep the worry under control if you know that it is still unlikely that you will be found to have a serious problem. The chart below shows what happens when 10,000 women are screened with breast X-rays.

Of every 10,000 women screened, only around 55 are found to have cancer and their chances of successful treatment are greatly improved because the cancer has been detected at a relatively early stage.

Mammography – the pros and cons

• **Just having the test makes you anxious**: Yes, but it doesn't last

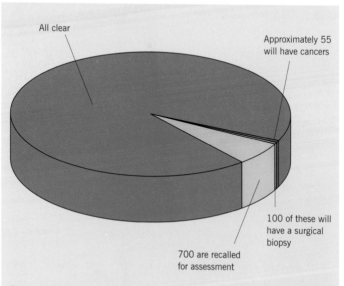

Of every 10,000 women given a mammogram, 700 will be recalled for assessment: 100 of these will have a surgical biopsy, of whom approximately 45 will be clear and 55 will have cancers

long and for the vast majority whose results are normal the relief makes it all worth while.

• **Supposing they miss something**: It is very uncommon for a tumour not to be detected by mammography in women over 50.

• **A positive result is worrying and means more tests**: Around one in 100 women screened get a so-called 'false-positive' result – this means that an abnormality is found which, after further investigation, is found not to be cancer.

• **The X-rays might be harmful**: Modern screening equipment delivers an extremely low dose of radiation and the chance that a mammogram could cause a tumour to develop is very small.

• **Why suffer the worry and discomfort**: On balance, the negative aspects of having a mammogram are very clearly outweighed by the real possibility that it could actually save your life. If you are one of the small minority of women whose mammogram does detect breast cancer, you will have a much better chance of successful treatment than if it were undiscovered and left to grow.

In those women who attend for screening, four of every ten women who would have died of cancer will survive.

KEY POINTS

✓ All women between the ages of 50 and 64 are currently invited every three years for breast screening, but by the year 2003 screening will be offered between the ages of 50 and 69

✓ Four of every ten lives lost to breast cancer can be prevented in this age group by attending breast screening

✓ After the age of 69, three-yearly screening is still recommended but you will need to make your own appointment

✓ Screening women under the age of 50 has not been shown to be cost-effective

Seeing the doctor

Whenever you experience any symptoms relating to your breasts, the first person to consult is your GP. His or her priority is to decide whether there is a chance that you might have some serious disease within the breast and, if not, whether the problem can be sorted out without referring you to someone else.

If you have a definite lump or your doctor wishes further advice, you'll be sent along to a hospital breast clinic. Alternatively, your GP may decide that your breasts should be checked again – perhaps at a different point in your menstrual cycle – and will ask you to come back for a follow-up examination.

The first person to consult is your GP.

THE BREAST CLINIC

The doctor will ask you to describe your symptoms in detail and also ask how long you have had them. If your problem is pain or a lump, he or she will also want to know if it varies in relation to your monthly cycle. You will then have a full examination. If you're seeing a male doctor, he will usually ask for a female nurse to be present during the examination.

Physical examination

The doctor will look at your breasts, first with your arms by your side, then above your head and finally with your arms pressing on your hips. By looking carefully at the outline of the breast in these various positions the doctor can often see changes in the outline of the breast which will help to identify the site and cause of any complaint. Next, your breasts are examined while you're lying flat with your arms folded underneath your head.

If, during this examination, the doctor finds a lump, he or she will concentrate on this area examining it with the fingertips and measuring the lump. After checking your breasts, the doctor usually examines the lymph glands in the armpit and those in the lower part of the neck.

Should you need any further investigations, the breast specialist who sees you will tell you exactly what tests are needed and explain why they are necessary.

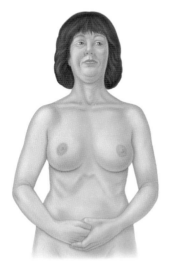
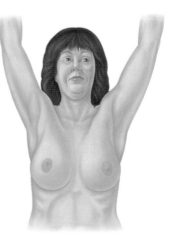

Arms to the side.   Arms over your head.

Breast examination by your GP.

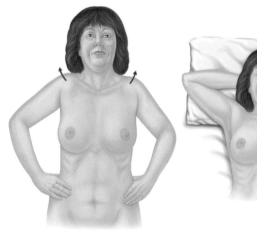
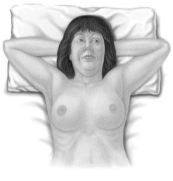

Arms on hips.

Lying down, arms folded underneath head.

Breast examination by your GP.

MAMMOGRAMS (BREAST X-RAYS)

If you're over 35 and haven't had a breast X-ray within the past year, the clinic doctor will probably send you to have one done. This X-ray is known as a mammogram. For more on what happens when you have a mammogram, see pages 7–9. Some breast units actually arrange for patients to have their mammograms before being seen by the doctor in the clinic so that the X-rays are on hand when you attend the clinic. Otherwise, the film will be ready for the doctor to examine within a few minutes.

ULTRASOUND SCANNING

X-rays do not pass easily through the breasts of women under the age of 35. This often makes it difficult to obtain images of sufficiently good quality because the breasts are too dense. Ultrasound, which is familiar to many women because it's used to look at babies during pregnancy, can also be used in the breast to tell whether a lump in the breast is filled with fluid (cystic) or whether it is solid.

Ultrasound is not useful as a screening test and is really only of value in patients where there is an abnormality on the X-ray or where there is a definite lump. When a lump is solid, ultrasound is an accurate means of judging whether it is benign and straightforward or whether it may be more serious.

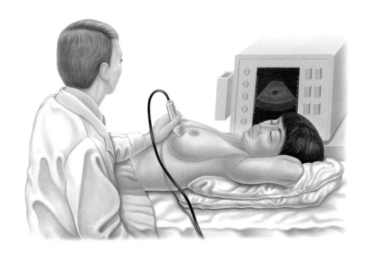

Ultrasound scanning.

NEEDLE TESTS

There are two types of needle test. One uses a small fine needle the same size as is used to take blood called fine needle aspiration; the second uses a slightly larger needle and takes a sliver or a little portion of tissue known as a core biopsy. Inserting a fine needle into a lump will show whether it is full of fluid (a cyst) or solid. The needle used for these tests is small – the same size as the ones used to take blood. As the breast is very sensitive, the needle test with the fine needle can be uncomfortable, but it doesn't take long to do. An alternative in solid lumps is to perform a core biopsy. Before this test is carried out, the skin and surrounding tissue are numbed with local anaesthetic. Provided that the local anaesthetic

has been injected in the right place, it is not a painful test. When the anaesthetic wears off, however, the area where the breast has been sampled can be tender and patients are usually advised to take painkillers, the same as those that are used for a headache, such as paracetamol or ibuprofen (Nurofen). After a core biopsy the area often looks quite bruised. This bruising tends to settle over a week to 10 days.

If the doctor who sees you is happy that there is no serious abnormality in your breast, then he or she will reassure you and tell you that you don't need to come back any more. If you have had a needle test or an X-ray, you may be given another appointment to come back for the results. In some clinics you

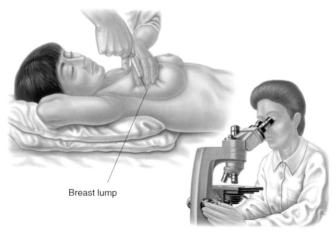

Breast lump

Microscopic examination of lump cells

Fine needle aspiration is a procedure used to withdraw sample cells from a breast lump, by inserting a small syringe needle directly into the lump.

may able to wait and get your results the same day.

As well as a doctor, you may also see a specialist breast care nurse while you're at the clinic. She will check to make sure that you understand what the doctor has told you and may help in arranging follow-up appointments and further tests.

Don't hesitate to tell her if you're worried about anything in particular or if you have any questions that have not been answered by the doctor. The nurse should have time to talk over your concerns and either be able to answer any questions you may have or to get the doctor to answer these questions for you.

FOLLOW-UP VISITS

You will be given a follow-up appointment if you need to come back to get the results of tests. If they indicate that there is no problem in the breast, then you won't usually need to see the doctor again. If, however, the tests suggest that the lump might be serious, the doctor will explain what this means.

Sometimes the results of the tests are such that it is not clear exactly what's wrong, in which case you may need to have further investigations.

If you have had a simple needle test, but this has not shown the cause of the lump, then it is possible that at your second visit you will have a core biopsy, which is described above.

Alternatively, a doctor may suggest that the lump is removed. This is called an excision biopsy and it can be performed either while you're awake, under local anaesthetic or more commonly under a general anaesthetic. Before any operation, you are asked to sign a consent form agreeing to the removal of the lump. It is important for you to know that the doctor performing the operation will only remove that lump and won't take any more tissue away without explaining the procedure to you first and getting your consent.

WHAT THE TESTS MEAN

Needle tests are very accurate and are rarely ever wrong if they show cancer. Occasionally, the mammo-gram or ultrasound scan will be reported as showing a cancer but, when it is tested with a needle or removed and analysed, it turns out to be non-cancerous.

This might happen in one out of 20 cases. This is why the doctor will often tell a woman that a lump might be cancer, but that it's impossible to be 100 per cent certain until it has been tested with a needle or removed and analysed.

The combination of performing a careful examination, doing X-rays and/or scans and removing cells with a needle for testing is very accurate and, if you have all these three tests, it is very rare to miss a cancer. If all the tests show that a lump is not serious, then it doesn't necessarily need to be removed.

KEY POINTS

✓ Your doctor will examine you if you report a breast problem. If the doctor wishes to obtain further advice you will be referred to a breast clinic

✓ At the breast clinic, you will be examined and may have the following done: a mammogram, a breast ultrasound scan or a needle test

✓ The combination of examination, X-rays or scans and a needle test is very accurate in identifying the cause of a breast lump

✓ Not all breast lumps need to be removed

Nature's mistakes

As we saw in the section on breast development on page 1, the ridge of tissue called the milk line normally disappears before birth. Occasionally, a part of the ridge which should have disappeared remains and forms an extra nipple or an extra breast. Extra nipples are common – between one and four in every 100 people have one. They are usually situated below the normal breast but above the umbilicus (belly button) on the milk line, while extra breasts are most common in the armpit. These extra nipples or breasts can occasionally be affected by the same diseases that affect ordinary breasts. An extra breast which is causing problems – whether physical or psychological – can be surgically removed but this is usually not necessary.

QUESTIONS OF SIZE

In theory, breast size doesn't matter at all; it has no bearing on a woman's sexuality or on her ability to breast-feed. In reality, however, concern about breast size is a source of very real distress to many women. It doesn't necessarily help them to know that breasts naturally come in many different shapes and sizes or that their own breasts are well within this normal range.

It is not at all unusual to have one breast noticeably larger than the other, with a bigger left breast being more common. The difference may not be obvious to anyone else, but, if the discrepancy is very marked, it can be corrected by surgery. Either the smaller breast can be made larger, or vice versa.

Very large breasts can cause their owners a lot of trouble. Apart from the embarrassment factor, which can make life particularly difficult for young women, large breasts may be painful. Their weight puts a strain on a bra's shoulder straps so they cut into the skin. Many women suffer a lot from backache as a result of large breasts. They get in the way of ordinary physical activity and can be a real handicap when it comes to games and sport.

Any woman troubled by difficulties like this should talk it over with her doctor. It may be worth considering surgery to reduce the size of her breasts. The operation, called reduction mammoplasty, can be done on the NHS and can make a very real difference to a woman's quality of life. It is not considered purely cosmetic surgery these days because the effect on a woman's physical and psychological well-being is often dramatic and very worth while.

Women considering the operation should be aware that they will be left with scarring on the skin around the nipple and underneath the breast, and that they are unlikely to have any nipple sensation afterwards.

Small breasts do not cause the same kind of problems as large ones, although individual women may be very concerned that their breasts are too small. However, it is extremely rare for surgery to increase breast size to be available on the NHS, so anyone who wants her breasts enlarged is likely to have to pay. The operation involves inserting implants behind the breast.

The most commonly used implants are made of silicone. There was a question mark over the safety of these silicone implants in the USA, but a team of British experts concluded that silicone implants do not cause any harm and that there is no reason for any women who have them to be concerned. An alternative to silicone is to use salt water implants, but these do not produce as good a result as silicone.

Even though the operation to enlarge breasts is not being done on the NHS, it is still worth asking your GP for advice if you are considering it as he or she may be able to recommend a good surgeon or clinic. It is possible to breast-feed after you have had breast implants. The most common complication after insertion of implants is the formation of capsules around them. The capsules contract down and result in hardening and this can cause pain, discomfort, change of shape and embarrassment. Rupture of the implants is a major concern among patients. The earlier varieties with thinner envelopes are particularly liable to rupture. In fact, ruptured implants cause very few problems because almost all the silicone remains within the fibrous capsule formed by the body. Newer implants are more robust and much less likely to rupture.

NIPPLES

Some women have naturally retracted or pulled in nipples which is not at all significant in health terms.

However, some women feel this is an embarrassing 'abnormality' and it can cause problems when it comes to breast-feeding. There is a device available from chemists, called Nipplette, which has been reported to be successful in resolving this in some women. It is possible to correct the problem with surgery, but, to pull the nipple out, the ducts behind the nipple usually need to be divided and this means that you are not able to breast-feed after this operation. When you are pregnant, wearing breast shells may encourage your nipples to protrude normally (see page 35).

Nipple piercing

This is now reasonably common. The problem is that the ring can cause damage to the ducts underneath the nipple, and this can result in recurrent infections or leakage of material from the duct through the skin. If this happens, the ring should be removed and the area allowed to settle. Occasionally infection does not clear up when the nipple ring is removed and an operation is needed. Very rarely, this can mean that the whole nipple itself needs to be removed.

MALE BREASTS

All men have some breast tissue under the skin and, like that of women, it does respond to hormonal changes, although much less dramatically. Other factors, including some medicines (see box on page 20) and occasionally other illnesses, may cause breast swelling (also known as gynaecomastia), but usually the situation resolves itself without the need for anything beyond a check-up.

Sometimes, a boy or a grown man may notice that he is starting to develop a breast shape that's more like that of a woman. It is actually not uncommon in boys between 10 and 16 years old – affecting between one- and two-thirds during puberty. It might seem alarming but is actually nothing to worry about at all and will almost certainly disappear quite naturally in time.

However, if it's noticeable enough to be really embarrassing or if the swelling hasn't begun to subside after two years, it's worth seeing your GP.

The same thing can sometimes happen in middle and later life, and a man between the ages of 50 and 80 who notices any breast swelling should tell his GP. Normally, no treatment is needed, but a mammogram may be necessary first to rule out any possibility of a malignant growth. One per cent of cancers in men are breast cancers.

DRUGS ASSOCIATED WITH ENLARGEMENT OF THE MALE BREAST (GYNAECOMASTIA)

Anabolic steroids	As used by body builders
Metronidazole	An antibiotic
Cimetidine Omeprazole Ranitidine	Used for stomach ulcers or heartburn
Amiodarone Captopril Digoxin Enalapril	Used for heart problems or hypertension
Diazepam Antidepressants Phenytoin	Used for anxiety or muscle tension
Alcohol Heroin Marijuana	

KEY POINTS

✓ Extra nipples and extra breasts are common

✓ Large breasts can cause considerable problems and surgery to make them smaller is available on the NHS

✓ Small breasts can be made larger using breast implants

✓ Enlargement of the breast, which can be embarrassing, is common in boys between the ages of 10 and 16, but usually disappears within a year or two

Breast pain

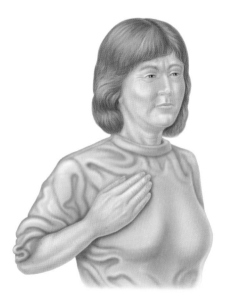

About five million women in the UK get breast pain, known medically as mastalgia. A survey carried out among women who work at Marks and Spencer found that 40 per cent had experienced breast pain recently and, of those with pain, just over one in five women said it had been severe.

More often than not, breast pain isn't that bad and many women simply accept it as a normal feature of the changes brought on by their menstrual cycle. As a general rule, we think of pain as a sign that there's something wrong, perhaps even a serious problem, but this is rarely the case with breast pain. Breast cancer is in fact usually painless. At one time it was thought that women who were worriers or who were depressed were more likely to complain of breast pain, but studies have now shown that there is no such connection.

IS THERE A PATTERN?

Breast pain can be divided into two types:

- cyclical – worse immediately before a menstrual period

- non-cyclical – where there is no association between the pain and the time of the month.

If you aren't sure whether your breast pain follows a regular pattern, it is worth keeping a diary for a couple of months. You could ask your GP to let you have one of the standard charts for recording breast pain, or simply make your own. On it, you need to note each day how bad the pain is (say on a scale from 1 to 5), and mark the days when you have your period. You could also record other details, such as any dietary changes, stressful events and so on. After a while, the diary should help you decide whether your breast pain is cyclical and whether there are other contributory factors for you.

CYCLICAL BREAST PAIN

Symptoms that come and go according to the time of the month are a familiar feature of many women's lives. You may become more aware of your breasts, perhaps because they feel full, heavy and uncomfortable or become lumpy and tender, usually around three to seven days before your period starts. Women who have got used to this often go to their GP because they begin to experience actual pain in the breasts before a period for the first time. This problem is more common in women in their 30s, but it can also happen in older women if they are taking hormone replacement therapy. Otherwise, it usually disappears after the menopause, but pregnancy or the Pill doesn't generally make any difference, and it can continue for many years.

You may find the pain isn't the same every month, but most women describe it as a heaviness or an ache, rather like toothache with the breast feeling tender when touched. It usually affects the outer half of the breast. Certain movements can increase the pain; this is particularly important if your daily life involves using your arms or lifting a lot. Unless they've experienced it for themselves, many people don't realise how bad breast pain can be or how seriously it can affect your life.

What causes it?

Despite the fact that cyclical breast pain occurs each month before a period, research has failed to show up any differences in hormone levels between women who experience bad breast pain and those who don't. Women with breast pain have been found to have some abnormality in the level of certain fatty acids in the blood. It may be that lifestyle factors – such as smoking, caffeine intake and diet – play a role, but what this might be is not yet clear.

Can treatment help?

Your GP will probably want to give you a thorough examination to make sure there is nothing obviously wrong. Most women with mild cyclical breast pain don't need any treatment as such, although it is worth seeing a trained bra fitter to make sure you are wearing the right size and type of bra – a firm, supportive bra of the kind recommended for sports wear can often relieve the pain.

Your doctor can also reassure you that cyclical breast pain has no connection with breast cancer – something which is at the back of many women's minds and naturally worries them. Mild breast tenderness which starts just before your period is due and disappears after it finishes is rarely, if ever, a symptom of any underlying disease.

Evening primrose oil

For a minority of women – about 15

per cent – the pain is so severe that it disrupts their lives and interferes with everyday activities. If you are one of these, there are various treatments your doctor will consider. He or she is most likely to suggest evening primrose oil to begin with. You'll probably be

prescribed six to eight capsules of Efamast 40 or three to four capsules of Efamast 80 to be taken every day for three months initially. This is long enough to assess whether you are one of the two-thirds of women whose breast pain does respond to treatment with evening primrose oil. If it is working, you should carry on with the capsules for another three months, then stop taking them. There is a 50 per cent chance that, when you stop taking the evening primrose oil, the pain will then have disappeared and will not return. If it does come back, again

HOW TO CHECK THE FIT OF A BRA

1. Make sure your bra fits around your body flat and is not too tight. Too tight a fit will be uncomfortable and could cause breathing difficulty. The bra should lie close between your breasts and not stand away from your body.

Typical well-fitting bra: straps not cutting in, cups full and lying flat on your body.

2. See that the bust is fully contained within each cup; sometimes gaping at the side means that the cup is too small. If the cup wrinkles all over it shows that the cup is too large.

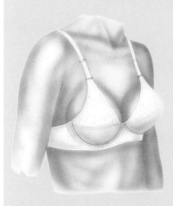

Cups not large enough, not in contact with your body.

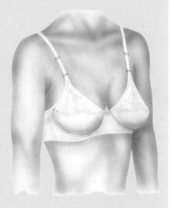

Cups too large, not filled adequately.

3. Check that flesh is not bulging over the top of the cups, under your arms and across the back. Is there flesh bulging beneath the band?

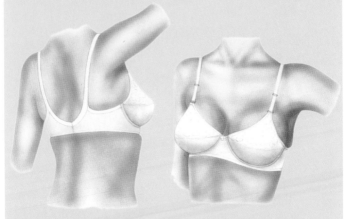

Is the band digging into your back?

Is flesh bulging out of the cups and under your arms?

4. If the bra is underwired, is the underwiring lying flat against your body, following the contours of your body and not digging into your breast? A soft cup bra will fit differently to an underwired bra, because the wire contains your breast whereas it can spread in a soft cup bra.

Is the underwiring comfortable and lying flat on your body?

HOW TO CHECK THE FIT OF A BRA

5. If your bust is heavy are the straps wide and strong enough to support it? Is the rest of the bra helping to support it?

Well-supported large bust.

Poorly supported large bust – straps digging in/poorly adjusted, cups too small for the task.

6. Is the cup 'spacing' correct? Do your breasts lie naturally, not pushed to one side or the other?

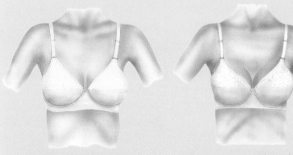

Correct cup spacing – breasts lying naturally.

Incorrect cup spacing – breasts pushed to one side.

7. Always test the fit of your bra both standing and sitting. The breast tends to 'plump up' when seated; this is especially noticeable in a strapless bra.

there's a 50 per cent chance that it will be much less severe than before. However, for the unlucky 25 per cent of women who find their breast pain is no better, another six-month course of Efamast may do the trick. Side effects with evening primrose oil are very few and minor (see box on page 29).

Other drug treatments

If evening primrose oil doesn't work and the pain is severe, there are other possible approaches to treatment. A variety of drugs is available which work by interfering with the hormones that act on the breast. They include danazol, bromocriptine and tamoxifen. Although they are sometimes more effective than evening primrose oil, they all have more side effects so it is important to weigh up the pros and cons with your doctor before starting to take any of them. However, it's worth remembering that any side effects will disappear once you stop the course of treatment. The side effects are summarised in the box on page 29.

• **Danazol**: Danazol is very effective in treating breast pain, and often works when evening primrose oil has failed and when the pain is very bad. Danazol works against the sex hormones, by blocking the release of two hormones from the pituitary; it reduces the amount of hormones produced by the ovaries and so reduces the amount of circulating oestrogen, which is thought to be one of the major hormones to cause breast pain. However, as with bromocriptine, you can't take it at the same time as the oral contraceptive pill and you must use a mechanical alternative, such as condoms, a coil or a cap.

• **Bromocriptine**: This drug is now rarely used in the treatment of breast pain because of its side effects. It works by reducing the amount of one of the hormones that acts on the breast – prolactin – which plays a role in production of milk. There is now a newer drug which reduces the amount of prolactin in the body, called cabergoline. This is taken once a week and as yet does not have a licence to be used in breast pain, but trials are in progress.

• **Tamoxifen**: Tamoxifen is used occasionally to treat severe breast pain. It interferes with the female hormone oestrogen, by stopping oestrogen reaching its target cells. It therefore has the same effect as danazol and reduces breast pain.

Other considerations

Although sometimes tried in the past, various treatments now known not to work include antibiotics, water tablets (diuretics) and vitamin

B_6. Although no particular oral contraceptive pill has been linked with breast pain, some women find it helps to change to a brand with a lower progestogen content. Others find the pain improves if they stop the Pill altogether and use an alternative means of contraception. Starting HRT can sometimes bring on breast pain and lumpiness which usually settles down after a while, but can remain a problem for some women. In these women, evening primrose oil is usually effective in controlling the pain and lumpiness.

How to help yourself
Keep a diary to record when your pain comes and goes and note down any factors that seem to play a part. Try the various strategies listed below one at a time and see if each one helps. If you try them all at once, you won't know which are responsible for any improvement.

- Get your bra size checked by a trained fitter; buy a couple of supportive, sports-style bras and, when your breasts are painful, wear one day and night

POSSIBLE SIDE EFFECTS OF MEDICATIONS

All the side effects of breast pain treatment are reversible – in other words, they disappear when you stop the treatment. You won't necessarily get any or all of them in any case, but you will need to talk over the balance of benefits and possible side effects with your doctor when deciding on the treatment that is best for you personally.

Treatment	Side effects
Evening primrose oil	Occasionally: stomach upsets, greasy skin and hair
Danazol	Oily skin, acne Occasionally: deepening of the voice
Bromocriptine	Nausea, giddiness
Tamoxifen	Hot flushes

- Start taking some regular aerobic exercise
- If you're a smoker, make up your mind to stop and do it
- Experiment with your diet: some women find that avoiding fried and fatty foods and drinks containing caffeine and cutting down on salt can all be helpful in relieving breast pain.

NON-CYCLICAL BREAST PAIN

Women who experience this type of breast pain tend, on the whole, to be older than those whose pain is cyclical, with an average age of 43. The pain of non-cyclical mastalgia can arise from the breast itself, from the muscles and ribs under the breast or from sites outside the breast.

You may feel it as one or more tender spots over your ribs, next to the breast bone or over the ribs just outside your breast. This type of pain actually comes from the muscles or ribs. It may be there all the time but, more often, it comes and goes without any regular pattern. Women usually describe the pain as burning or drawing, but it can sometimes be stabbing in nature.

Can treatment help?

Before the doctor can offer you any treatment, he or she needs to identify where precisely your pain is coming from. If the source can be pinpointed to a specific area on the chest wall as is often the case, you may be given either an anti-inflammatory cream or gel to rub in or an injection of a local anaesthetic and a steroid.

Non-cyclical pain coming from the breast itself is often eased by a simple pain-killer, such as ibuprofen. It can also help to wear a well-fitting supportive bra day and night. If these simple measures don't help, your doctor may think it worth while trying you on evening primrose oil (Efamast capsules, see page 24). Although they don't work as well as for women with cyclical breast pain – only about half as many respond to treatment – they have very few side effects. The drug treatments used for cyclical breast pain, such as danazol, can also be tried in extreme cases, but they don't work as often for non-cyclical pain and of course they have more side effects than evening primrose oil (see page 29).

KEY POINTS

✓ Breast pain is very common

✓ It is not a frequent symptom in women with breast cancer

✓ Wearing a firm supporting bra can help relieve the pain

✓ Pain that comes and goes in relation to the menstrual cycle usually responds to treatment with evening primrose oil

✓ Hormone replacement therapy can cause breast pain in older women

✓ Pain that is not related to the menstrual cycle is best treated by simple pain-killers

Breast infection

This most often affects women between the ages of 18 and 50, but is much less common than it used to be. Although they can occur at any time, many breast infections happen while a woman is breast-feeding her baby.

BREAST-FEEDING

Infection is most likely to be a problem during the first six weeks of breast-feeding, although some women develop it while they're weaning their babies. Although it can be treated effectively, it is far better to prevent it altogether if possible. If you are having any problems getting your baby to breast-feed happily and comfortably, don't hesitate to ask the advice of your midwife, health visitor or a breast-feeding counsellor. The first symptoms of a breast infection are pain, swelling, redness and tenderness and you may start to feel quite unwell, with a raised temperature, general aches and pains and a headache, almost as though you had flu. You may well have been aware before the infection set in of a cracked nipple or a break in the nearby skin. If you have also had a problem with one of your breasts becoming engorged because the milk wasn't being drained properly, this makes an infection more likely; this happens because the milk flow normally washes away any harmful organisms which doesn't occur when there is reduced flow of milk. Many mothers find their babies feed more easily from one breast rather than the other – often the left breast if she's right-handed and vice versa. This may mean the other, less popular breast is not completely emptied and so is more prone to engorgement and infection.

If you suspect you have developed an infection, you should see your doctor as soon as you can.

You'll probably be given a prescription for one of the antibiotics which can be taken safely while breast-feeding. It is important that you carry on feeding your baby from the infected breast as draining the milk from it completely will reduce the chances of an abscess forming. Your baby won't come to any harm from the bacteria in your milk as they will be easily killed off by the acid in his or her stomach. If you can't carry on feeding for any reason, you should express the milk from the infected breast, either by hand or using a breast pump.

If the infection does not settle quickly on antibiotics, then it is likely that an abscess has formed and your GP will send you to hospital to have it drained. This can usually be done in the outpatient clinic using a local anaesthetic, but occasionally it may need a general anaesthetic, although this isn't ideal when you have a young baby to look after. These days, the draining may well be done using a fine needle to withdraw the contents of the abscess (localised collection of pus). This procedure, called aspiration, may need to be carried every two to three days until there is no more pus in the abscess. Occasionally the abscess itself is very close to the skin; rather than drain it with a needle, a small cut is made in the skin and this allows the pus to drain out. Once the abscess

has been aspirated or drained, you can carry on with breast-feeding.

OTHER BREAST INFECTION

Women who aren't breast-feeding sometimes develop an infection, usually in an area of the breast close to the nipple. Most of them are in their late twenties or early thirties and around 90 per cent are smokers! It seems that something in cigarette smoke somehow damages the major ducts beneath the nipple and the damaged area then becomes infected. The condition, known as periductal mastitis, causes pain and redness in the area around the nipple and sometimes there'll be an underlying lump.

Normally, antibiotics get rid of the infection, but, if not, then an abscess has probably developed. When this happens, you will have to go to hospital to have the abscess drained – see above.

Unfortunately, because draining the abscess does not remove the damaged duct, you are quite likely to find the problem recurs. Sometimes, the duct is so severely damaged that a hole develops which allows fluid from the duct to leak through the skin stopping it from healing. This condition is known as a mammary duct fistula. If you develop this problem or suffer repeated bouts of infection, you may need a small operation to remove the damaged ducts and solve the problem for good.

It's not unknown for a woman to develop an infection in another part of the breast, away from the nipple, although it is not as common. However, when it does happen, this type of infection usually responds well to treatment with antibiotics.

SKIN INFECTIONS

Some women who have large breasts may find the skin underneath their breasts becomes infected. This happens because the skin of the breasts is in permanent contact with the skin of the chest wall or abdomen, which produces heat and sweating. This makes the skin an ideal breeding ground for bacteria which then set up an infection.

Usually the problem can be treated with an antibiotic either orally or as a cream that you rub into the affected area. You'll be advised to keep it as clean and dry as possible. This means washing twice a day and dabbing the skin gently dry with a cotton towel or using a hair dryer instead. You should avoid using talc or body lotion and either opt for cotton bras or wear a cotton T-shirt or vest inside the bra next to the skin. If the cream and hygiene measures don't work, it may mean you have a deeper infection which will need treatment with antibiotics in tablet form. If you are overweight, you can reduce the chances of the infection recurring by losing weight. However, if you are normal weight but simply have very large breasts, it may be worth considering whether you could benefit from surgery to make them smaller (see page 18).

KEY POINTS

✓ Breast infection during breast-feeding is now uncommon but can be a problem during the first six weeks

✓ If you suspect that you have an infection, visit your GP as soon as possible for antibiotics. You can continue to breast-feed even if you are taking antibiotics

✓ Infection around the nipple in non-pregnant women is usually associated with smoking

Nipple problems

Problems with nipples are relatively common, but fortunately most of them are not at all serious.

SHAPE MATTERS

Some people have nipples that are naturally retracted or pulled in which isn't at all important unless you want to breast-feed, when it can cause difficulties. It often helps to wear breast shells inside your bra while you're pregnant as this will encourage your nipples to protrude and make feeding your baby easier.

If your nipples change shape and become indrawn or pulled to one side as you get older, you should let your doctor know. Although this may prove to be just a normal feature of ageing, it is important to get it checked.

As you get older, the ducts underneath the nipple become shorter and they pull in the middle part of the nipple, often producing a slit effect across the nipple. The ducts also widen with age and can fill up with a cheesy material that can leak out on to the surface of the nipple. Your doctor will probably want you to have a check-up at a breast clinic, where you will be examined and have a breast X-ray to make sure everything is normal and there is no lump behind the nipple.

A pulled-in nipple may be a sign of inflammation of the ducts underneath the nipple, particularly in younger women.

For women whose nipples change shape or become indrawn, a mammogram is usually necessary to exclude the possibility of cancer. Once any serious underlying disease has been ruled out, however, you can be reassured that the change in your nipple shape is nothing to worry about.

NIPPLE DISCHARGE

A discharge usually comes through the nipple from the ducts underneath, but it may sometimes come from the surface of the nipple itself. The word discharge sounds like something unpleasant but, in fact, two-thirds of women who are not pregnant can be made to produce fluid from the nipple simply by cleaning it and massaging the breast. A common form of discharge is milky discharge which can continue to leak from the breasts long after a woman has finished feeding her baby – perhaps for months or even for years. Much more rarely, a woman may start to produce milk from her nipple even though she isn't and hasn't ever been pregnant.

All women, even if they have never been pregnant have fluid inside their breasts, but it doesn't normally find its way to the outside because the ducts are blocked with plugs of a substance called keratin. Vigorous exercise or sexual activity may dislodge these plugs and so release fluid in a discharge which comes and goes. The fluid, which may come from one or both breasts, usually only appears in small amounts and may range in colour from white to pale yellow to green to blue/black. In all cases, it is perfectly normal and nothing to worry about.

Discharge which is a symptom of duct disease tends to be more troublesome, appears in larger quantities and is there all the time. A yellowish or blood-stained discharge is most likely to be caused by a wart, known as a papilloma, in one of the ducts underneath the nipple. Discharges that are blood-stained, persistent or troublesome are easily treated by removing the abnormal duct. This is a very simple operation performed through a very small incision around the nipple, and it is very successful at getting rid of the discharge.

A thicker, cheesy discharge also occurs in older women whose ducts widen with age and become filled with cheesy material which can leak onto the surface of the nipple.

It is also possible to have a discharge from the skin surrounding the nipple rather than from the nipple itself. Some women have trouble with eczema on the nipple and the skin around it. Although the cause isn't clear, the treatment is simple – using a very dilute steroid cream.

Another possible cause of discharge from the nipple is a disease of the skin of the nipple known as Paget's disease. This causes an ulcer on the surface of the nipple and is usually a sign that there is a cancer or pre-cancer present in the breast. As a result of this, women with discharge from the surface of the nipple or from the surrounding skin need to have a careful breast examination, plus mammograms and, if necessary, samples of skin and tissue from your breast may be taken for microscopic examination. If tests show Paget's disease, then an operation is usually required. The operation can either be removal of the nipple and tissue underneath the nipple, sometimes followed by radiotherapy, or it can be treated by a mastectomy.

KEY POINTS

✓ Problems with the nipples are common

✓ Pulling in of the nipple can be the result of infection, ageing or cancer

✓ Most discharge from the nipple is not serious

Lumps and cysts

Most breast lumps are not cancerous. In fact, all women have lumpy breasts, and many of the lumps that women find are just lumpy areas of normal breast tissue which become more prominent and are often easier to feel just before a period is due.

Lumpy breasts used to be known as fibrocystic disease, but now lumpy breasts are considered normal and women with lumpy breasts are not more likely to develop breast cancer. Only if you notice a new, distinct and separate lump do you need to report it to your doctor.

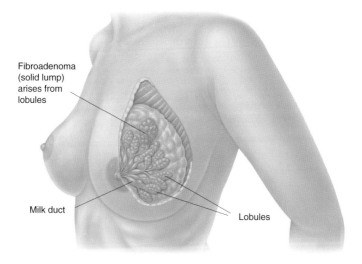

Fibroadenoma (solid lump) arises from lobules

Milk duct

Lobules

Fibroadenoma.

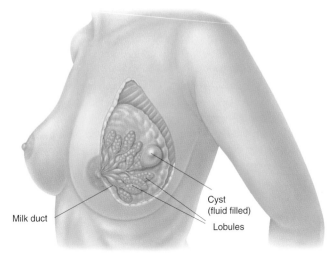

Milk duct

Cyst
(fluid filled)

Lobules

Breast cyst.

FIBROADENOMAS

These lumps aren't strictly speaking a disease at all; rather they are overgrowths of the 'leaves' described on page 3 – the breast lobules. They account for six out of ten lumps found in women under the age of 30 and four out of ten in women between the ages of 20 and 30; they become less common later in life. Ultrasound and fine needle aspiration or core biopsy (see pages 12–13) are usually used to confirm the diagnosis, but once your doctor is sure that the lump is a fibro-adenoma you may not need any actual treatment. At least one in three will get smaller or disappear on their own within two years, but if you're worried or if the lump is getting bigger you can opt to have it removed.

CYSTS

Cysts are swollen lobules which can form as breast tissue ages, which is why they mostly affect women in their 30s, 40s and 50s. They are especially common in the years before the menopause. We don't know what causes cysts, but it is not just a blockage of the draining duct.

Most cysts are smooth, mobile lumps; some are large enough to be easily visible and they can be painful. It is usually quite easy to identify a cyst with ultrasound and mammography. Not all cysts need to be aspirated but, if a cyst is large and causing pain and discomfort, the final and definitive investigation of aspiration is conveniently also the treatment for these cysts. The doctor inserts a fine needle into the lump, with no anaesthetic, and extracts the fluid from inside the cyst and usually the lump disappears completely. The fluid may be yellow, green or blue/black. If the fluid is blood-stained it will be sent for tests because, very occasionally, a cancer may form in the wall of a cyst, but this is rare. Cysts that produce blood-stained fluid are usually removed.

Of every six women who develop a cyst, half will never have another one. Two will have between three and five cysts during their lifetime and the remaining woman will have more than five. The good news is that it is not necessary to have a cyst drained every time, provided the doctor is confident that it is a cyst rather than a solid lump.

Women who have had one or more cysts are not at significantly increased risk of developing breast cancer (there is some risk but the risk is not considered to be significant).

KEY POINTS

✓ Most lumps are not cancerous

✓ The most common cause of a lump in a young woman is a fibroadenoma

✓ Fibroadenomas do not need to be removed

✓ Cysts are more common in women in their 30s, 40s and 50s, and are treated by needling of the lump and removing the fluid

✓ Benign lumps are not associated with a significantly increased risk of breast cancer

Breast cancer

More women get breast cancer than any other type of cancer – between one in 12 and one in 10 will develop breast cancer at some point in their lives and the incidence is set to increase over the next decade. A woman's risk of developing breast cancer doubles every ten years, and it is actually very rare in younger women. Despite its relative rarity in younger women, it is the most common cause of death in women between the ages of 35 and 50, although it is true that many women, including women under the age of 50, are successfully diagnosed and treated. It is also worth remembering that seven out of eight breast lumps are found to be benign – in other words, they are non-cancerous. Of those that do turn out to be malignant, the earlier they are detected and treated, the better the woman's chances of survival.

WHY IS CANCER A PROBLEM?

A lot of cells in the human body are growing at any one time, but their growth is very carefully controlled so that the number of cells that are produced matches the number of cells that are dying. A cancer is a group of cells that are growing and dividing at a faster rate than cells are dying, so that the group of cells that form the lump gets bigger and bigger. As the lump increases in size, so some of the cells develop the ability to move away from the lump and get to other parts of the body through the bloodstream. This is called spread (metastasis) of a cancer and some of the cells that get into the bloodstream start to form new lumps in different areas of the body. If the cancer cells grow in important areas, such as the lungs, the liver or the brain, or if the cells involve a lot of different bones, then this can cause major problems.

WHO GETS BREAST CANCER?

It isn't a simple matter to try and work out your personal level of risk because so many factors play a part in determining who gets breast cancer. In any case, an individual has little or no control over most of the risk factors. What you can do if you face a higher than average risk is to take advantage of screening programmes and visit your doctor promptly if you suspect you may have a problem.

Even if you know you are more susceptible to breast cancer than the next woman, any lump you find is still more likely to be benign than malignant.

Experts have worked out some of the factors which seem to make it more likely that a woman may develop breast cancer, but it's worth bearing in mind that, even if all of them were relevant to one particular woman, she still might not get the condition!

- **Getting older**: More women in older age groups develop breast cancer, with a doubling of risk every 10 years.

- **When your periods begin and end**: Starting early and going on beyond the age of 55 seem to be linked with increased risk.

- **Postponing pregnancy**: Women who don't become pregnant until after the age of 30 or who never have children are at greater risk than those who are pregnant for the first time in their teens although, of course, this is not in itself a good reason for getting pregnant in your teens!

- **Breast-feeding**: A woman who has breast-fed one or more children has a lower risk than a woman who has never done so.

- **Abnormal breast cells**: A few women who have had a non-cancerous condition are found to have an abnormality in certain breast cells which makes later cancer more likely. Although this is not common, a woman with this problem, known as atypical hyperplasia, will need regular check-ups. Other types of non-cancerous breast problems do not increase your risk of developing cancer.

- **Overweight**: Being seriously overweight, greater than 1.5 times the average weight for your height, when you are older (postmenopausal) does increase breast cancer risk. There is also a link between breast cancer and eating a diet that's high in fat, but no one is yet sure quite how this operates.

• **Drinking and smoking**: Some studies have shown a link between drinking alcohol and breast cancer, with women who drink a lot having a higher risk than those who either drink no alcohol or drink it in moderation. Smoking has not been directly linked to breast cancer risk, but its implication in other diseases and effects on your general well-being cannot be over-emphasised.

• **Taking the Pill**: There is a very slightly increased risk for women while they are taking oral contraceptives. The risk is short-lived and disappears ten years after stopping the Pill.

• **Taking hormone replacement therapy**: The major benefits of hormone replacement therapy (HRT) are in controlling menopausal symptoms such as hot flushes and night sweats. HRT also protects against osteoporosis, but only when taken for many years. There are some concerns about the use of HRT because it does increase the risk of breast cancer, strokes and blood clots. The risk of breast cancer is greater the longer you take HRT and the risk appears to be greatest for women who take combined oestrogen and progestogen preparations, especially when the progest-

ogen is taken continuously, compared with women who take oestrogen HRT alone. HRT can also cause breast pain and can interfere with the ability of breast screening to detect small cancers.

The decision whether to take HRT is an individual one, based on the pros and cons for each individual woman. There are also options for some women other than oestrogen. Hormone replacement therapy is usually only given to a woman with a strong family history of breast cancer if she is having severe menopausal symptoms that are not controlled by other non-hormonal drugs.

• **Family history**: Up to one in ten women who develop breast cancer have inherited some kind of genetic abnormality which makes them more susceptible to the condition. There are various ways of identifying women with this kind of risk – see the box on 'Breast cancer families' (pages 44–5).

As you can see there is not much anyone can do to avoid many of the risk factors. However, it is worth trying to get your weight down if you need to and cutting down on fat in your diet as this will also reduce your risk of developing heart disease.

MAKING THE DIAGNOSIS
The first indication that something is

A woman may develop breast cancer because of some abnormality in her genetic make-up inherited from one of her parents, in which case other members of her family will have been affected too. Her genetic risk is increased if:

- several members of her family have or have had breast cancer;

- she has relatives who developed breast cancer while under the age of 50: the earlier in life it happened, the greater the risk that it was caused by an inherited abnormality;

- she has relatives who have had cancer in both breasts or who have had certain other types of cancer, particularly cancer of the ovaries, colon and prostate, while young, which can be caused by the same gene.

If you are seeing your doctor about a breast problem and know that several members of your family have had cancer, not just breast cancer, it is important to find out as much as you can about what happened. It would be useful to know what type of cancer they had, at what ages they developed it and, if relevant, at what ages they died.

Cancer genes can be inherited from either parent, even though neither of them may have actually developed cancer themselves. No one yet knows how many breast cancer genes there are, but five have been identified so far. About one in three cases of inherited breast cancer is thought to be due to an abnormality in a gene known as

BRCA-1, and the same proportion to another gene called BRCA-2, with the other three genes and a number of undiscovered genes being responsible for the rest. At the moment, testing for abnormal genes is available only in certain centres, but the number of centres is set to increase over the next few years.

Before any woman can be offered a test, it is necessary for the doctor to show that somebody in the family who had breast cancer had an abnormal gene. Women who come from such affected families may then be given the opportunity to find out if they are carrying the abnormal gene and are at increased risk. Women who carry an abnormal gene have between a 60 per cent and 85 per cent chance of actually developing breast cancer at some time in their lives. Women in these families also have a higher risk of ovarian cancer.

Before opting for the test, women should be aware that the finding of an abnormal gene could make it difficult to obtain life assurance (and maybe a mortgage). This is why women having the test are offered counselling before and after it.

If, having had the test, a woman is found to be carrying an abnormal gene, then she may wish to take steps to reduce the risk of breast cancer actually developing. Usually this will mean starting regular intensive screening at an earlier age, or alternatively a woman whose family history suggests that she is very high risk, or whose gene test shows that she is carrying an abnormal gene, can opt for a double mastectomy and breast reconstruction or can enter one of the ongoing drug prevention studies to try to prevent breast cancer developing.

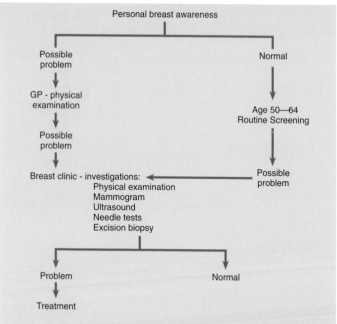

Personal breast awareness

Possible problem — GP - physical examination — Possible problem

Normal — Age 50—64 Routine Screening — Possible problem

Breast clinic - investigations:
Physical examination
Mammogram
Ultrasound
Needle tests
Excision biopsy

Problem — Treatment

Normal

The cycle of personal breast awareness and routine screening is the key to the early detection of any possible problems, more detailed examination of the breasts and early treatment for any disorder.

wrong may be the woman herself noticing a lump or change in a breast or it may be picked up by her GP or at a routine mammogram. It is very important for you to be aware of how your breasts normally feel and look so that you will spot any change quickly. Of course, you must follow up any such observation by going to your GP.

If you find a lump or other abnormality in your breast you are bound to be worried, but the sooner you get it checked out, the better.

The chapter 'Seeing the doctor', on page 10, explains in detail what happens when you go to your GP and what tests may be required when you have a breast problem which needs investigation (see pages 11–15). As a reminder of the way things usually work, the flow chart summarises the various stages you might go through.

KEY POINTS

✓ Breast cancer affects one in ten women in the UK

✓ The incidence of breast cancer doubles every ten years of a woman's life

✓ Up to ten per cent of women who develop breast cancer have inherited an abnormal gene which puts them at increased risk of developing this condition

✓ Women at high risk are usually offered screening, starting at a younger age

✓ Genetic testing is becoming more widely available but is not easy to perform

✓ HRT does slightly increase the risk of developing breast cancer; the risk becomes significant in women taking long-term (> 5 years' use) HRT and also appears to be greater for combined oestrogen and progestogen preparations, particularly when both hormones are given continuously

Different kinds of breast cancer

Many people don't realise that breast cancer is not just one disease which is always treated in the same way and which has the same predictable outlook for everyone who gets it. There are several aspects of the disease which play a part in determining how well the person will do and whether her outlook is likely to be better or worse.

Factors which must be taken into consideration include the size of the tumour, whether it is the type which has the potential to spread outside the breast, what the tumour looks like under the microscope and so on.

ASSESSING THE PROBLEM

Breast cancers develop from the cells that line the breast lobules and the draining ducts. Cancer cells that are confined to the lobule and the ducts are called 'in situ' or 'non-invasive'. They are also sometimes referred to as 'pre-cancers', in recognition of the fact that they do not have the ability to spread to other parts of the body which most people associate with cancer. An invasive breast cancer is one where the cells have moved beyond the ducts and lobules into the surrounding breast tissue. Non-invasive cancer can turn into invasive cancer if left in the breast untreated. Invasive cancers do have the ability to spread and they are able to enter lymph channels in the breast and spread to the lymph glands under the arm – this is the most common place that they spread to or from which they can get into the bloodstream and spread elsewhere in the body. The lymph system is involved in fighting infection and is a network of lymph channels and lymph glands throughout the body. If a germ gets into the body, it passes through the lymph channel to the lymph glands where the cells that are involved in the killing of germs are stored. Cells in the lymph glands either themselves kill the germs or produce substances called 'antibodies' which are released into the bloodstream. The lymph glands that drain the breast are under the arms, so when the cancer cells get into the lymph channels they move to these glands.

Both non-invasive and invasive cancers are also further subdivided according to other criteria. In the case of invasive cancers, the most important distinctions are in the different ways they grow and spread and the type of cells involved.

When a cancer is examined under the microscope, it may be possible to assess how aggressive it is likely to be – in other words how far and how fast it is likely to spread. Following this type of analysis, a tumour may be assigned to one of three grades – ranging from grade I to grade III in order of seriousness.

Rather than being one disease, breast cancer is in fact a whole lot of separate diseases. It may be easier to understand if you think of breast cancer in terms of dogs: at one end of the spectrum is a small cancer of a so-called 'special type' of low-grade (I) cancer which behaves much like a small, well-trained family pet. At the other extreme is a large cancer consisting of cells of no special type which are grade III and behave more like an uncontrollable rottweiler. The aim is always to find out what type of tumour an individual has and tailor the treatment to suit the cancer.

One more thing doctors need to know before treatment can be started is whether the cancer has spread and, if so, how far. If breast cancer is diagnosed, you will normally have a thorough clinical examination, blood tests and a chest X-ray to check that there is no evidence of cancer elsewhere in the body and to ensure your general fitness for surgery.

Occasionally, the doctor may decide to do a bone scan to check all your bones and a liver scan to look in detail at your liver. This information allows the doctor to assess the stage of the cancer and the best way to treat it.

This process is known as 'staging' the cancer, and distinguishes three main groups.

- **Early**: Cancer that seems to be confined to the breast and/or the lymph nodes of the armpit on the same side of the body.

- **Locally advanced**: Cancer that has not apparently spread beyond the breast and armpit but is best not treated initially by surgery. In locally advanced breast cancer, the skin of the breast is usually abnormal and is either swollen or red, or the cancer is growing directly into the skin. These cancers used to be treated by surgery first, but it was found to be successful only in about half of all patients; in the others the cancer came back in the areas next to where the surgery was performed.

• **Advanced**: Cancer that has spread beyond the breast and armpit to other parts of the body.

KEY POINTS

✓ There are many different types of breast cancer

✓ Cancer cells confined to lobules and breast ducts are called in situ or pre-cancer

✓ The most common site for an invasive cancer to spread is the lymph nodes under the armpit

Treating breast cancer

Once a thorough assessment has been made, it's then possible to work out the most appropriate treatment. This might include surgery, radiotherapy, hormone therapy, chemotherapy or a combination, depending on the cancer itself and taking into account the individual woman's wishes. When the possible options have been explained to you, you will be invited to share in the decisions about what is to be done, although of course some women prefer to leave such decisions to their doctors.

In most cases, treatment is likely to involve surgery alone or surgery and radiotherapy to deal with the cancer in the breast and the glands under the arm, followed by drug treatment aimed at destroying any undetected cancer cells which may have escaped into other parts of the body.

Of all cancers, breast cancer is one of the most treatable cancers and is associated with a high cure rate. Treatments for breast cancer are improving and so is survival. Despite the fact that more women develop breast cancer every year, the number of women who actually die from breast cancer is falling, which demonstrates the effectiveness of current treatments.

SURGERY

When the lump is relatively small (under four centimetres in size), it is usually possible for the surgeon to remove it along with a small amount of the surrounding tissue (breast-conserving surgery or lumpectomy). With a larger lump, this breast-conserving operation may not be worth while because so much of the breast would have to be taken away to get rid of the cancer. In some women with

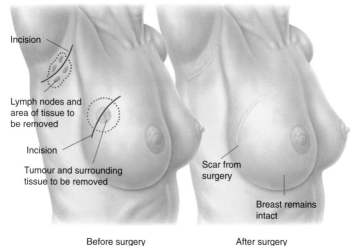

Incision

Lymph nodes and
area of tissue to
be removed

Incision

Tumour and surrounding
tissue to be removed

Scar from
surgery

Breast remains
intact

Before surgery   After surgery

Breast-conserving surgery.

relatively small breasts, who have lumps under four centimetres in size, then sometimes when the lump and some surrounding tissue are taken away it may not be possible to leave enough breast tissue to make saving the breast worth while.

In fact, about one in three breast cancers can't be removed in this way, and are best treated with mastectomy – an operation to remove the whole breast, usually including the nipple. Fortunately, surgical technique has improved dramatically since the days when a so-called radical mastectomy – removing all the tissue right down to the chest wall – left the woman with a serious deformity of the chest and arm and damaged her ability to use her arm normally. You may

know, or be told about someone to whom this has happened, but there is no cause to worry that the same thing might happen to you if you need to have a mastectomy. These days, some women actually choose to have a mastectomy even though they could have a simple lump removal.

There are also situations where a woman with a lump smaller than four centimetres may be advised to have a mastectomy. The main ones are:

- When there is more than one lump in the breast. Research shows that, even if all these lumps are removed, other cancerous lumps are quite likely to develop later in other parts of the same breast.

- When the cancer is directly under the nipple so that it would have to be removed at the same time. Rather than leave the breast without a nipple, it is sometimes better, although not always necessary, to take the breast away altogether and have a breast reconstruction – see page 55.
- Sometimes, an operation to remove the lump is not entirely successful, because either some cancer or pre-cancer is left behind. Another operation to remove more tissue may solve the problem but it might be necessary to remove the whole breast.
- Sometimes, the tissue surrounding the lump may be abnormal

and on its way to becoming cancerous. If it can't all be removed by a lumpectomy, a mastectomy may be the safest option.

When you have either breast-conservation surgery or a mastectomy, the surgeon usually removes some or all of the lymph glands from under your arm. There are about 20 of them and they are the most common place to which the breast cancer may spread. Knowing whether this has happened and, if so, how many of these axillary glands are affected is important both in assessing the severity of the cancer and in deciding on the best type of drug treatment. If the surgeon just needs to see whether

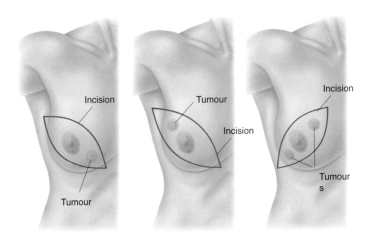

A mastectomy is an operation to remove the whole breast, usually including the nipple.
A surgeon will attempt to remove the minimum amount of tissue to get rid of the cancer.

the cancer has moved into these glands, removing either a single gland that drains the cancer or a few of them is usually sufficient, but the only way to find out how many have been affected is to remove all of them.

Sentinel nodes

The first lymph node draining the site of the cancer is known as the sentinel node. Identification of the sentinel node is performed by injecting radioisotope and blue dye around the tumour. The radio-isotope is injected either the night before or the morning of surgery and a sentinel node(s) can be visualised in almost nine of ten patients having a scan. The blue dye is injected immediately before operation and allows the surgeon to see the sentinel nodes as they are coloured blue. Where tests on one or only a few of the glands removed during surgery show that they have been affected by cancer, the remaining lymph glands need to be treated by surgical removal or radio-therapy. In any case, most women will have a course of radiotherapy after breast-conservation surgery even if the glands aren't affected (see the section on radiotherapy, page 57).

Sometimes, surgery in the armpit can cause damage to the nerves in the upper arm so it feels numb afterwards. This is obviously a nuisance but often improves with time. Around one in 20 women who have all their lymph glands

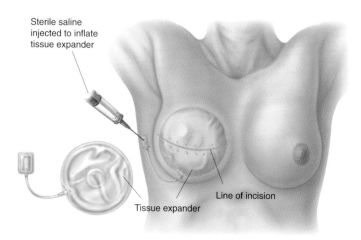

Sterile saline injected to inflate tissue expander

Line of incision

Tissue expander

After breast surgery, a patient may choose reconstructive surgery. One option involves inserting an implant under the skin. This is expanded over several months by injecting saline into it.

removed or who have had them treated with radiotherapy develop lymphoedema or swelling in the arm. Treatment can usually reduce the problem, although it can't always be got rid of completely. Massage can help, as can wearing an elastic stocking and it's worth propping your arm up on several pillows while you're sitting down. It's also important to avoid injuries or infection in your hand – from gardening, for example – as this can leave you with worse swelling even after the infection has cleared.

Treating locally advanced breast cancer

Locally advanced breast cancer is usually treated initially by drug treatment. In patients with a cancer that is hormone sensitive (oestrogen receptor positive), hormone therapy is usually given but, in oestrogen receptor-poor or -negative cancers and particularly if the breast is swollen, red or oedematous (inflammatory cancer), chemotherapy is used first. The most common hormone drugs used are the aromatase inhibitors (anastrozole or letrozole) or tamoxifen in older patients and goserelin (an ovarian inactivator) plus tamoxifen in younger women. After hormone or chemotherapy has shrunk the tumour, this is usually followed by a combination of surgery and/or radiotherapy.

Treating breast cancer that has spread

Few other cancers when they spread have such a variable course. Patients with breast cancer that has spread can live for many years. This is particularly true for patients who have hormone-sensitive breast cancer. The aim of treatment is to produce effective control of symptoms with minimal side effects. Both hormonal therapy and chemotherapy are widely used. In premenopausal women with hormone-sensitive breast cancer (oestrogen receptor positive), ovarian inactivation combined with either tamoxifen or one of the new aromatase inhibitors is the most commonly used treatment. In postmenopausal women, one of the new aromatase inhibitors, either letrozole or anastrozole, is now the most commonly prescribed treatment. For patients with cancer that has spread to bone, local radiotherapy is effective at treating localised bone pain. Drugs called bisphosphonates are also used to treat bone disease. These are bone-strengthening agents and they reduce the ability of the cancer cells to cause bony damage.

BREAST RECONSTRUCTION

If you have decided with your doctor that your cancer is to be treated with a mastectomy operation, the surgeon will probably discuss with you the possibility of having breast reconstruction surgery done at the same time. The operation is often more successful if done straight away rather than if it is left until months later. There is no evidence that immediate recon-struction makes a recurrence of cancer any more likely nor that, if it should come back, it will be harder to detect.

How is it done?

The simplest method is to insert an implant under the skin, but this usually needs to be combined with some means of stretching the remaining skin to make up for the amount that was removed during the mastectomy operation. This may be done in two stages, so that the skin is expanded before the implant is inserted or a combined expander and implant can be used. The idea is that the expander is gradually inflated with injections of fluid over a period of months to stretch the skin, in much the same way as the growing fetus stretches the skin of a woman's abdomen during pregnancy.

When this process is complete and the skin has expanded enough, the device can either be removed and replaced with a permanent prosthesis or implant or some fluid can be removed leaving the smaller, breast-sized implant in position.

Most implants consist of a plastic (Silastic) shell or envelope filled with silicone gel. Older implants had a very thin shell and small amounts of silicone would occasionally leak out of these. Newer implants have a much thicker outer shell and are much less likely to leak any silicone. The body produces tissue around an implant, called a capsule and, even if the implant does leak silicone, in all but a few women the body contains all the silicone within this capsule. Very occasionally, the silicone can leak into the surrounding tissues and causes irritation and scarring. Many medical devices placed into the body contain silicone and these include artificial joints and heart valves. Any silicone that gets into the bloodstream can occasionally find its way to other parts of the body, but even at this stage it doesn't seem to cause significant problems. There is, for instance, no evidence now that silicone, when it leaks, causes joint problems or any other disease. Alternative implants are available which contain salt water, but these do not give such good results. Around one in ten women experiences problems with implants because the capsule around the implant tightens or hardens and causes the implant to change shape, and this may be painful.

The original implants had a

smooth surface, but the newer implants have a rough, irregular (textured) surface and these textured prostheses are associated with a much lower incidence of hardening.

Occasionally infection may develop, although the chances are considerably reduced by giving the woman antibiotics during and after the operation.

An alternative to using artificial implants alone is to bring skin and muscle from another part of the body to replace the lost breast. This may be taken from the back or from the abdomen. When the 'back flap' method is used, a muscle called the latissimus dorsi is chosen and an implant is usually needed in addition to the muscle to create the appropriate size of breast. Sometimes it is possible to transfer fat with or without muscle from the abdomen. This is called a 'TRAM flap' (transverse rectus abdominus myocutaneous flap). With a TRAM flap, an implant is not usually necessary. Removal of muscle from the lower part of the abdomen can be minimised by a careful technique of isolating the blood vessels that supply the skin and fat – the so-called 'de-ep flap'. These blood vessels are then re-connected to vessels under the arm to keep the flap alive.

The main disadvantage of using muscle flaps or a de-ep flap is that the transplanted tissue does not always survive. About one in 100 back flaps and one in 20 to 30 TRAM or de-ep flaps fail for this reason.

Whether the surgeon uses muscle or an implant to reconstruct the breast, it is possible to reconstruct a nipple at a later time. This is done either by transplanting some darker coloured skin from the upper inner thigh or by tattooing the skin to create an areola. Alternatively, a simpler solution is to opt for one of the very natural-looking stick-on nipples now available.

RADIOTHERAPY

There is good evidence to show that all women who have had breast conservation surgery do benefit from radiotherapy treatment afterwards but it is only needed in about a quarter of patients after a mastectomy.

Radiotherapy kills cells that are growing. In a normal breast, only a few cells are actually growing at any one time, but a cancer consists of cells that are growing all the time. Radiotherapy, therefore, has its greatest effects on cancer, although it inevitably produces some slight damage to other tissues which can result in slight scarring of the breast.

How is it done?

You will probably be asked to come to the outpatient clinic each

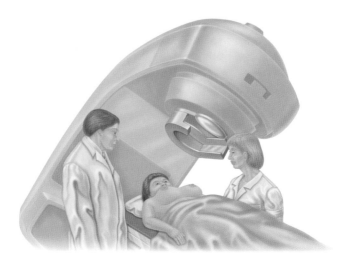

Radiotherapy.

weekday for four or five weeks to have the radiotherapy. It only takes a few minutes each time and is completely painless. It's a bit like having an X-ray and you don't need to worry that it will make you radioactive – it won't! Before you're given the first dose, the area to be treated is marked on your skin using a semi-permanent dye. This is so that whoever is giving the treatment can be sure you are in exactly the same position each time and you will be asked to keep absolutely still while it's being done.

After a few days of radiotherapy, your skin may look red and feel a bit sore, rather like you've spent too long in the sun. Towards the end of treatment you can also get some blistering of the skin. As when you put water onto sunburned skin, it can make the skin sore, some radiotherapists prefer patients to keep the treated areas dry and just to apply creams. Other doctors are quite happy for you to get this area wet. You should follow the advice given by your own radiotherapist as he or she will have decided what is best for you. You should also protect the treated area from the sun.

Nowadays, there are very few side effects from radiotherapy, for instance it doesn't make your hair fall out and it doesn't make you sick, although towards the end of the treatment you can feel slightly tired. Some patients who get radiotherapy to the breast do get a slight cough and this is caused by the fact that when you give radiotherapy to the breast you also give some to part of the lung immediately under the breast. This can cause slight scarring of the lung which causes irritation and results in a cough or, very occasionally, you might be slightly breathless. There are specific treatments for this, so if you experience these problems just report them to your own doctor.

FOLLOW-UP APPOINTMENTS

If you've had breast conservation surgery, you'll probably have to go for a check-up every six months for the first year and then for a yearly check. You'll have mammograms of both breasts every one to two years indefinitely. If you've had a mastectomy, you will have check-ups for the first five years. You will also have mammograms of the other breast every one to two years indefinitely.

DRUG TREATMENT

An advantage that drugs have over other kinds of treatment such as surgery and radiotherapy is that drugs reach all parts of the body. This means that they can act on cancer cells which have spread but in such small numbers that they can't be detected. As a result, they can prevent cancer recurring for months or even years after treatment. If cancer is already widespread by the time it is first diagnosed, drugs may be the only practical way of treating it.

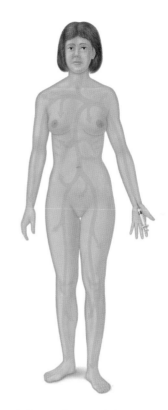

Anti-cancer drugs can destroy cancer cells that have spread throughout the body.

The drug treatment used for breast cancer falls into two main categories: hormones and chemotherapy.

Hormones

Most breast cancer is affected by hormones, and mainly by oestrogen. The other natural hormones that affect breast cancer are progestogens. At low levels they don't seem to have much influence, but, when given to patients at high doses, progestogens can make breast cancer shrink as effectively as any other hormonal manipulation, such as removing oestrogen or by using anti-oestrogens (see later).

It is possible to determine whether a tumour is sensitive to hormones by doing a chemical test on tumour specimens, taken at biopsy. Most breast cancers are oestrogen sensitive. There is a tendency, however, for younger patients to have a slightly higher incidence of hormone-insensitive cancers and a tendency in older patients (women after the menopause) to have a high incidence of hormone-sensitive cancers.

- **Oestrogen-sensitive tumours**: In women who have passed the menopause, about 80 per cent have oestrogen-sensitive tumours, but the proportion goes down to 60 per cent of younger premenopausal women. These hormone-sensitive cancer cells have receptors on their surfaces which react to oestrogen,

SIDE EFFECTS OF HORMONE TREATMENTS	
Hormone therapy	**Side effects**
Ovarian inactivation*	Menopausal flushes and sweats, joint stiffness, lower libido and vaginal dryness
Tamoxifen	The effects above plus weight gain, transient nausea, effects on the eyes, endometrial cancer risk, thromboembolic complications
Specific aromatase inhibitors	As for ovarian inactivation plus nausea and muscular and joint pains
Progesterone	Increase in appetite, weight gain, vaginal bleeding, thromboembolism

*This can be ovarian ablation, a surgical procedure, or inactivation by drugs. Both involve lower levels of oestrogen being produced by the body.

called oestrogen receptors, and oestrogen binds to these receptors causing the cells to multiply and grow more quickly. Tamoxifen is a drug that works by stopping the oestrogen getting to the oestrogen receptor. In some patients this results in tumour shrinkage, in others in prevention of further growth of the tumour. Either of these effects can be of great benefit in controlling the disease and removing the symptoms of the cancer. The effect of tamoxifen may last for many months or years in individual patients, although it is impossible to predict how long the effect can last.

The only serious side effect is that tamoxifen can double the incidence of endometrial cancer in the lining of the womb in post-menopausal women. There is no doubt that this risk is over-emphasised in the media and the actual risk is very low. Most of the evidence suggests that the optimum length of time to take tamoxifen is probably five years for protection against breast cancer.

Other drugs

A new and increasingly used class of drugs for treating breast cancer, called the aromatase inhibitors, has recently become available and they are proving to be very beneficial treatments. Basically, they are used in women who are postmenopausal

and they act by blocking the production of oestrogen which is still made in considerable quantities in these women. In blocking the production of oestrogen they deprive any breast cancer cells of oestrogen which acts as a stimulant. This is the only way that their action is similar to the effect of tamoxifen, but they can work after tamoxifen if this has failed to control the tumour. They are so well tolerated that they are now being used as alternatives to tamoxifen in the treatment of early disease. There are three new aromatase inhibitors that are available, and these are anastrozole (or Arimidex), letrozole (or Femara) and exemestane (or Aromasin).

Progestogens are also used to treat breast cancer in a number of patients and most often used after initial therapy with tamoxifen, and one of the new aromatase inhibitors, has failed. The mechanism of action of progesterone is complex and poorly understood, but the drugs do have a very good track record over many years for controlling the disease.

The main reasons why tamoxifen or the aromatase inhibitors are chosen ahead of the progestogens are the side effects. These are mild or minimal with the former but can be more troublesome, with weight gain being the major problem, with high-dose progestogens.

A glance at the box on page 60

gives some insight into the most common side effects seen with hormone therapy, and which drugs are particularly associated with those side effects.

Chemotherapy

This treatment involves being given a combination of anti-cancer drugs, often three at a time. The prime target for such drugs is meant to be identifying and killing cells that are actively growing and dividing. Unfortunately, anti-cancer drugs are not able to recognise cancer cells specifically and they will kill other actively dividing cells such as cells of the blood or bone marrow (and hair).

The bone marrow is an extremely important tissue in the body because it produces the blood cells and the cells of the immune system which fight infection. Drugs that destroy these cells result in complications such as anaemia, tendency to infection, and problems with clotting resulting in a tendency to bleed after minor trauma.

The main problems with the blood, however, concern the white cells which are part of our defence against infection; there is such a big turnover in the number of white cells in the blood that they are particularly sensitive to the damage caused by toxic chemotherapy drugs. The art and science behind successful cancer chemotherapy is the combination of drugs used

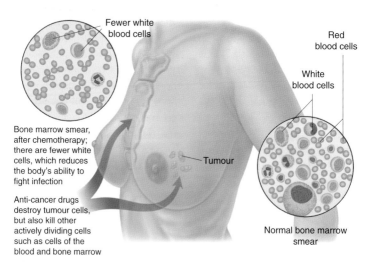

Fewer white blood cells

Red blood cells

White blood cells

Bone marrow smear, after chemotherapy; there are fewer white cells, which reduces the body's ability to fight infection

Anti-cancer drugs destroy tumour cells, but also kill other actively dividing cells such as cells of the blood and bone marrow

Tumour

Normal bone marrow smear

Chemotherapy involves taking a combination of anti-cancer drugs, often three at a time. The anti-cancer drugs also damage the bone marrow and white cells in the blood, which are part of our defence against infection.

which minimises the damage to the blood and maximises the damage to the cancer cells.

Sometimes chemotherapy is given before surgery in order to shrink the tumour so the surgeon can leave more of the breast undamaged.

Cancer chemotherapy is usually given through an intravenous drip into your arm. It can be done on an outpatient basis. Treatments vary but each session usually takes about half an hour and is repeated every three weeks. Some people prefer to stay the night in hospital after a treatment session, especially if they are very anxious. They may well be frightened of having chemotherapy because they have heard that there are very nasty side effects, such as nausea, vomiting and hair loss. In fact, by no means everyone will experience all or even any of these problems. Some of the anti-cancer drugs now cause little or no hair thinning and anti-nausea medicines given with the chemotherapy work very well. You can be given a sedative and/or anti-nausea drug through a drip if necessary.

One of the less well-known side effects of chemotherapy is to cause premature menopause in women who are still menstruating. This is particularly likely to occur in women in their late 30s and 40s, but even younger patients can temporarily have cessation of their periods as a result of the effects of chemotherapy on production of hormones by the ovaries. Typically, what happens in younger patients is recovery of periods after chemotherapy, but even then the natural menopause that follows may be brought forward by several years. All this indicates is that, except in the youngest patients, chemotherapy is likely to impair fertility and some women who have delayed having children take active steps to attempt egg storage before chemotherapy, so that they have the possibility of having a family after the breast cancer has been treated. The most reliable way to achieve this is to be seen by a specialist in infertility medicine and probably to undergo storage of fertilised eggs (in vitro fertilisation or IVF). Experimentally, some units are now looking at the storage of unfertilised eggs but at the moment this is an unproved technique and unreliable. Not all women undergoing chemotherapy have their fertility impaired, so it is advisable that they avoid becoming pregnant by using barrier techniques such as the condom because contraceptive pills can have an adverse effect on the breast cancer.

- **Intensive chemotherapy**: It was thought for some patients that ordinary chemotherapy was not

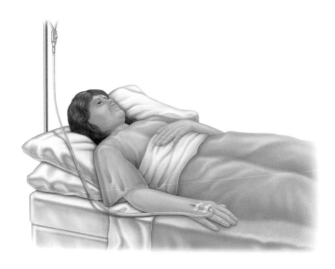

Anti-cancer drugs administered through an intravenous drip.

adequate, especially when the tumour was thought to be particularly aggressive. Studies have been carried out using very high doses of chemotherapy, which destroy the cells in the person's bone marrow, so before the chemotherapy, healthy cells are removed from the bone marrow, stored and then given back afterwards. Results of trials of this technique carried out in Europe and the USA have not shown any advantage for this method of treatment.

TREATING NON-INVASIVE OR *IN SITU* CANCER

Two main types of non-invasive (*in situ*) cancer can be recognised from the pattern of cells and the type of cells. Ductal carcinoma *in situ* is the most common form of non-invasive cancer and now makes up 20 to 25 per cent of screen-detected 'cancers'. Treatment of ductal carcinoma *in situ* (DCIS) involves surgical removal of all the disease in the breast. This can usually be achieved by breast-conserving surgery or lumpectomy, although sometimes mastectomy is required. After breast-conserving surgery, current evidence suggests that most patients benefit from a course of radiotherapy. The role of tamoxifen in the treatment of non-invasive cancer is unclear, but some patients do appear to gain some benefit from it.

The other type of carcinoma *in*

situ is much less common and is called lobular carcinoma *in situ* (LCIS). This abnormality identifies patients at increased risk of breast cancer, which means that they need to be kept under careful review. Treatment usually consists of follow-up with regular mammograms at yearly intervals. There is some evidence that patients with this condition benefit from tamoxifen, and ongoing studies in the UK are investigating this.

MENOPAUSAL SYMPTOMS AND HRT

Both chemotherapy and hormone therapy can produce menopausal symptoms and may indeed artificially induce permanent menopause. Many patients ask whether it is possible just to take HRT to relieve the unpleasant symptoms of the menopause. The advice at most centres is not to take HRT until alternatives have been tried, although the facts are that no one knows whether HRT adversely affects the breast cancer or not. The problem is that HRT is made up of low doses of oestrogen which, in theory, can stimulate some forms of breast cancer to grow again. Trials are being undertaken to see whether HRT can be used safely but the answers will not be available for some years. There are other ways of alleviating the menopausal symptoms caused by anti-cancer treatments, sometimes involving drugs such as low dose progestogens and certain types of antidepressants Sometimes trying to alter lifestyle such as wearing clothes that tend to reduce sweating (loose and made of natural, rather than synthetic, fibres) also helps.

COMPLEMENTARY MEDICINE

Most doctors are concerned about the idea of people with breast cancer opting solely for alternative medicine when their disease is so eminently sensitive to conventional treatment. Nevertheless, many people find great comfort in having some input into the control of their condition by visiting herbalists or other practitioners of so-called natural medicines.

The commonsense approach is to discuss this openly and honestly with your GP. He or she is unlikely to raise any objections, provided that you don't opt for complementary medicine instead of conventional treatment.

NEW DEVELOPMENTS

There has been increasing interest in new treatments, including new chemotherapy drugs and immunotherapy using antibodies targeted against cancer cells. The most promising new chemotherapy drugs are the taxanes (Taxol and Taxotere) which are derived from the bark of the yew tree. These drugs have shown very encouraging results in advanced breast cancer. They are being evaluated in early disease and further trials are ongoing. Although they are more effective, they do produce slightly more side effects.

An antibody that has been raised against a target on the surface of some aggressive breast cancer cells, herceptin, is now available and has shown very encouraging results when given alone or combined with chemotherapy in patients with a certain type of breast cancer that over-expresses a protein called Her2neu or erbB2. About 20 per cent of cancers over-express this protein, and this over-expression is more common in the cancers of younger women.

WHEN A CURE ISN'T POSSIBLE . . .

Despite the best efforts of the medical and surgical teams, some women with breast cancer will go on to develop advanced disease which can't be cured. Even when this does happen, however, there is still an enormous amount that can be done to help both the woman herself and her family.

It is nearly always possible to control symptoms such as pain and nausea and the palliative care team can advise either the GP or the hospital oncology department about the optimum use of drugs such as pain killers, drugs that combat nausea and diarrhoea, and how to maximise the patient's appetite, which can often be poor as a result of the illness or the treatment. It should be remembered that the main aim of the intervention on behalf of the palliative team is to give the patient the best possible quality of life with the minimum symptoms of the disease and the minimum side effects of treatment.

For more information about organisations which can provide information and support in this situation, see pages 70–1.

KEY POINTS

✓ There is a variety of hormonal agents very effective for treating hormone-sensitive breast cancer

✓ Chemotherapy doses and schedules are optimised to give the best anti-cancer effect while causing the minimum damage to the normal tissues

✓ Palliative treatment of breast cancer is often done in conjunction with an expert care team whose aim is to improve the patient's quality of life

Personal reactions

Any breast problem, even one which is minor in health terms, is likely to affect a woman psychologically and emotionally as well as physically. Very many women are sensitive about the shape and size of their breasts and of course breasts are an important aspect of any woman's sexuality. Both men and women perceive breasts in that way and a woman may be concerned about her partner's likely reaction to any breast problem, as well as her own. From her own perspective, anything being wrong with her breasts may have a damaging effect on her self-image and so take on an importance way beyond its significance in pure health terms. Of course, no two women will react in exactly the same way and your reaction to any breast problem is unique, but knowing that these kind of worries are normal may help to keep them in proportion.

Doctors and nurses who treat women with all kinds of breast problems are well aware of the psychological aspects of breast disease. Usually, they will ask about your emotional reactions and whether you have any worries you would like to talk over and it really is worth taking the opportunity to raise anything that's on your mind. Some people find this difficult, perhaps feeling that nothing can be done to help or that they would be wasting the professionals' time. This is very much not the case, and keeping your concerns to yourself is likely to do more harm than good in the long run.

You should be offered support and advice by the doctors and nurses involved in your care, but there are also numerous support groups which can offer something more for those who want it. In particular, there is a lot of help available for women who have breast cancer and their families, including the opportunity to meet and to talk to others in a similar situation. This is usually someone who has had breast cancer treated successfully and has some training in helping other people cope. More details can be found in the next section.

When it is a member of your family or close friend who has a serious condition such as breast cancer, it can be hard to express your worries or seek emotional support for yourself. It's easy to believe that you shouldn't compete with the patient's needs for help even though you will have your own concerns and worries, and many of the self-help groups also provide support for people in this situation.

Many relatives believe that they must not compete with the patient's need for help, even though they may have as many or more concerns. There are now groups to help relatives cope with breast cancer.

KEY POINTS

✓ Breast conditions can often affect women psychologically and emotionally

✓ Do not keep your concerns to yourself but share them with your carers

✓ Support should be available from your doctors and nurses, and is also available from self-help groups

Useful addresses

SUPPORT GROUPS

If you would like to talk to someone else who has been through similar experiences, trained volunteers can be contacted through Breast Cancer Care (see below) or local self-help groups. The following national associations provide emotional support and practical help to women with breast cancer or to their friends and relatives.

Breast Cancer Care

Kiln House
210 New Kings Road
London SW6 4NZ
Freephone: 0808 800 6000
Tel (admin): 020 7384 2984
Fax: 020 7384 3387
Email: bcc@breastcancercare.org.uk
Website: www.breastcancercare.org.uk

Specialist breast care nurses provide practical advice, medical information and support to women concerned about breast cancer. Volunteers who have had breast cancer themselves assist in giving emotional support to cancer patients and their partners. Free leaflets and a prosthesis-fitting service are also provided.

Cancerlink

11–21 Northdown Street
London N1 9BN
Freephone Support Link: 0808 808 2020
Groups Line: 020 7520 2603 (training, information and development for cancer self-help and support groups)
Admin: 020 7833 2818
Fax: 020 7833 4963
Email: cancerlink@cancerlink.org.uk
Website: www.cancerlink.org

Has now become part of Macmillan Cancer Relief (see below). This is for any individual with cancer, not just women with breast cancer. Their information service offers support and can help anyone given options for treatment by providing information that allows you to make an informed decision.

CancerBACUP

3 Bath Place
Rivington Street
London EC2A 3JR
Cancer Support Service:
Information: 020 7613 2121
Tel: 020 7696 9003 (booklets about
different types of cancer and
treatments)
Freephone: 0808 800 1234
Website: www.cancerbacup.org.uk

Provides advice and information about all aspects of cancer as well as emotional support for cancer patients and their families. There is a very wide range of free publications on a large number of different cancers, treatments and related issues. The Information Service is staffed by a team of specially trained nurses and supported by a panel of medical specialists. There is also a free and confidential counselling service.

Cancer Research UK

61 Lincoln's Inn Fields
London WC2A 3PX
Tel (information nurses): 0800 226 237
or 020 7269 3142
Tel (admin): 020 7242 0200
Fax: 020 7269 3100
Email: customer.services@cancer.org.uk
Website: www.cancerresearchuk.org

Funds research into cancer and education. Provides information to people with cancer and their carers.

Macmillan Cancer Relief

89 Albert Embankment
London SE1 7UQ
Information line: 0808 808 2020
Tel: 020 7840 7840
Fax: 020 7840 7841
Email:
informationline@macmillan.org.uk
Website: www.macmillan.org.uk

A national charity dedicated to improving the quality of life for people with cancer, and their families. It funds Macmillan Nursing Services, for home care, hospital and hospice support. Financial help is also given. Incorporates Cancer-link (see above).

Marie Curie Cancer Care

89 Albert Embankment
London SE1 7TP
Tel: 020 7599 7777
Fax: 020 7599 7788
Email: info@mariecurie.org.uk
Website: www.mariecurie.org.uk

National charity which runs ten specialist palliative care hospices around the UK. Provides a national palliative care nursing service. Is involved in research and in the education of healthcare professionals in a range of cancer and palliative care programmes.

SOCIAL SECURITY BENEFITS

Details of social security benefits for women are available by contacting:

National Association of Citizens Advice Bureaux
115–123 Pentonville Road
London N1 9LZ
Tel: 020 7833 2181
Fax: 020 7833 4367
Website: www.nacab.org.uk

or look in the local telephone directory or library for the address of the nearest Citizens Advice Bureaux. There are 1,500 bureaux nationwide and all of these can provide free, impartial, confidential advice and help. Most specialist units have access to support funds and can help people who want to apply.

THE INTERNET AS A SOURCE OF FURTHER INFORMATION

After reading this book, you may feel that you would like further information on the subject. One source is the internet and there are a great many websites with useful information about medical disorders, related charities and support groups. Some websites, however, have unhelpful and inaccurate information. Many are sponsored by commercial organisations or raise revenue by advertising, but nevertheless aim to provide impartial and trustworthy health information. Others may be reputable but you should be aware that they may be biased in their recommendations. Remember that treatment advertised on inter-

national websites may not be available in the UK.

Unless you know the address of the specific website that you want to visit (for example, familydoctor. co.uk), you may find the following guidelines helpful when searching the internet.

There are several different sorts of websites that you can use to look for information, the main ones being search engines, directories and portals.

Search engines and directories

There are many search engines and directories that all use different algorithms (procedures for computation) to return different results when you do a search. Search engines use computer programs called spiders, which crawl the web on a daily basis to search individual pages within a site and then queue them ready for listing in their database.

Directories, however, consider a site as a whole and use the description and information that was provided with the site when it was submitted to the directory to decide whether a site matches the searcher's needs. For both there is little or no selection in terms of quality of information, although engines and directories do try to impose rules about decency and content. Popular search engines in the UK include:

google.co.uk
aol.co.uk
msn.co.uk
lycos.co.uk
hotbot.co.uk
overture.com
ask.co.uk
espotting.com
looksmart.co.uk
alltheweb.com
uk.altavista.com

The two biggest directories are:

yahoo.com
dmoz.org

Portals

Portals are doorways to the internet that provide links to useful sites, news and other services, and may also provide search engine services (such as msn.co.uk). Many portals charge for putting their clients' sites high up in your list of search results. The quality of the websites listed depends on the selection criteria used in compiling the portal, although portals focused on a specific group, such as medical information portals, may have more rigorous inclusion criteria than other searchable websites. Examples of medical portals can be found at:

nhsdirect.nhs.uk
patient.co.uk

Links to many British medical charities will be found at the Association of Medical Research Charities (www.amrc.org.uk) and Charity Choice (www. charitychoice. co.uk).

Search phrases

Be specific when entering a search phrase. Searching for information on 'cancer' could give astrological information as well as medical: 'lung cancer' would be a better choice. Either use the engine's advanced search feature and ask for the exact phrase, or put the phrase in quotes – 'lung cancer' – as this will link the words. Adding 'uk' to your search phrase will bring up mainly British websites, so a good search would be 'lung cancer' uk (don't include uk within the quotes).

Always remember that the internet is international and unregulated. Although it holds a wealth of invaluable information, individual websites may be biased, out of date or just plain wrong. Family Doctor Publications accepts no responsibility for the content of links published in their series.

Index

CELTIC

THE OFFICIAL HISTORY

Brian Wilson spent eighteen years as Labour MP for Cunninghame North and served in five UK Ministerial capacities. On leaving politics in 2005, he became a Non-Executive Director of Celtic plc. He lives on the Isle of Lewis.